DK SUPER World

MEXICO

Discover Mexico's vibrant culture,
ancient ruins, golden beaches,
and delicious cuisine

PRODUCED FOR DK BY

Editorial Caroline Wakeman Literary Agency
Design Collaborate Agency
Graphic Story Illustrator Matt Garbutt

Senior Editor Amelia Jones
Senior Art Editor Gilda Pacitti
Managing Editor Katherine Neep
Managing Art Editor Sarah Corcoran
Production Editor Robert Dunn
Production Controller Rebecca Parton
Publisher Sarah Forbes
Managing Director, Learning Hilary Fine

First American Edition, 2025
Published in the United States by DK Publishing,
a division of Penguin Random House LLC
1745 Broadway, 20th Floor, New York, NY 10019

Copyright © 2025 Dorling Kindersley Limited
25 26 27 28 29 10 9 8 7 6 5 4 3 2 1
001–345901–Jul/2025

All rights reserved.
Without limiting the rights under the copyright reserved above, no part of this publication may be reproduced, stored in or introduced into a retrieval system, or transmitted, in any form, or by any means (electronic, mechanical, photocopying, recording, or otherwise), without the prior written permission of the copyright owner.

Published in Great Britain by Dorling Kindersley Limited

A catalog record for this book is
available from the Library of Congress.
HC ISBN: 978-0-5939-6653-2
PB ISBN: 978-0-5939-6652-5

DK books are available at special discounts when purchased
in bulk for sales promotions, premiums, fund-raising,
or educational use.
For details, contact: DK Publishing Special Markets,
1745 Broadway, 20th Floor, New York, NY 10019
SpecialSales@dk.com

Printed and bound in China

www.dk.com

CONTENTS

MAP — 4
Mexico

FACT FILE — 6
All About Mexico

TERRAINS — 8
Deserts, Caves, and Rainforests

LANDMARKS — 10
Chichén-Itzá

FLORA AND FAUNA — 12
Sacred Creatures and Adapted Animals

CULTURE — 18
People, Sports, and Entertainment

RELIGION — 22
Blending of Beliefs

NATIONAL HOLIDAYS AND FESTIVALS — 24
Family, Fun, and Fiestas

FOOD AND DRINK — 26
Mexican Menus

RECIPE — 28
Chilaquiles

HOME, WORK, AND SCHOOL — 30
Living, Learning, and Earning

SCHOOL DAY DIARY — 32
Amada's Day

HISTORY — 36
Civilizations and Civil Wars

QUETZALCŌĀTL AND THE LEGEND OF MAIZE — 38

VOCABULARY BUILDER — 42
A Day in Tenochtitlán

GLOSSARY — 44

INDEX — 46

Words in **bold** are explained in the glossary on page 44.

# MAP

MEXICO

Mexico is a vast land dominated by **deserts** in the north, hills and **mountains** in the middle, and **tropical** forests in the south. Some of the biggest ancient **civilizations** lived in the region of Mexico, such as the **Maya** and **Aztec empires**. Ruins of the ancient cities are still visited today. Mexico is split into 31 states and 1 federal district, which is where the government is based.

FASCINATING FACT!

Mexico is the birthplace of chocolate! The Olmec and Maya civilizations were the first to transform cacao plants into something like the chocolate we have today. They made a bitter drink called *xocolatl*.

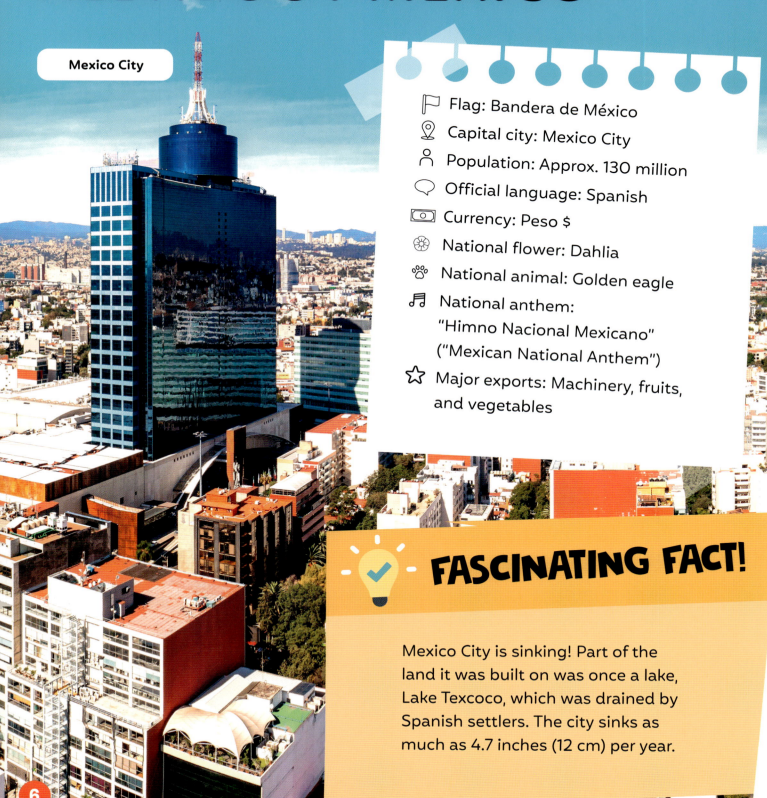

FACT FILE

ALL ABOUT MEXICO

Mexico City

- 🏳 Flag: Bandera de México
- 📍 Capital city: Mexico City
- 👤 Population: Approx. 130 million
- 💬 Official language: Spanish
- 💵 Currency: Peso $
- ❀ National flower: Dahlia
- 🐾 National animal: Golden eagle
- 🎵 National anthem: "Himno Nacional Mexicano" ("Mexican National Anthem")
- ☆ Major exports: Machinery, fruits, and vegetables

FASCINATING FACT!

Mexico City is sinking! Part of the land it was built on was once a lake, Lake Texcoco, which was drained by Spanish settlers. The city sinks as much as 4.7 inches (12 cm) per year.

Ruins of Tenochtitlán in Mexico City

Capital city
Before Mexico City existed, the Aztec people built the city of Tenochtitlán in the same spot in the 1300s. This was the base of their empire. When the Spanish invaded, they destroyed Tenochtitlán and built a new city there.

Eagle and snake
The Mexican flag is inspired by the Aztec legend of the city of Tenochtitlán: the god Huitzilopochtli told his people to make their home wherever they saw an eagle perched on a cactus eating a snake.

Languages
While the most common language spoken in Mexico is Spanish, the government also recognizes at least 63 **Indigenous** languages. The two most-commonly spoken of these are:

Náhuatl, spoken by the **Nahua** people (1.7 million speakers)

Yucatec Maya, spoken by Maya people in the Yucatán Peninsula (800,000 speakers)

FIND OUT!

Mexico borders the United States of America in the north and Guatemala and Belize in the south. Do you know which continent it is on?

Answer: North America

TERRAINS

DESERTS, CAVES, AND RAINFORESTS

Mexico's landscape contains mountains, deserts, **volcanoes**, and beautiful coasts. Much of the north is dry and **arid**, while the south becomes more tropical and even supports rainforests.

Volatile volcanoes
The Trans-Mexican Volcanic Belt is a chain of volcanoes that goes from west to east across Mexico. There are more than 20 volcanoes, some of which are still active today. The most volatile volcano is Popocatépetl in Central Mexico, which has been spewing towers of ash since 1994.

Popocatépetl

FASCINATING FACT!

In one Aztec legend, the volcanoes Popocatépetl and Iztaccíhuatl were two humans who fell in love and turned into mountains when they died.

8

Diverse desert

The Chihuahuan desert covers nearly 250,000 square miles (647,500 sq km). It is cooler than most deserts and gets more rainfall. Because of this, it is one of the most biodiverse deserts in the world. However, it is threatened by human population growth, bad water management, and overgrazing by farm animals.

Forests in the sky

The cloud forests in the Yucatán are so called because they are located at high altitudes and are often shrouded in fog. They are very wet! Because of their unique climate, cloud forests are home to rarely seen animals, including unusual butterflies, ocelots, and the vibrant quetzal.

Underground caves

A cenote is a kind of underground cavern filled with water with an opening at the top. Cenotes are formed when rain dissolves soft limestone and creates a hole that fills with water. As the cave gets bigger, the roof collapses, forming a cenote. Many ancient societies considered cenotes sacred.

LANDMARKS

CHICHÉN-ITZÁ

Chichén-Itzá was once the capital city for the Maya peoples. It was the trading center for gold, food, stonework, and other goods. Up to 50,000 people lived there. Now, the ruins of the city are a major archaeological site and it is considered one of the new seven wonders of the world.

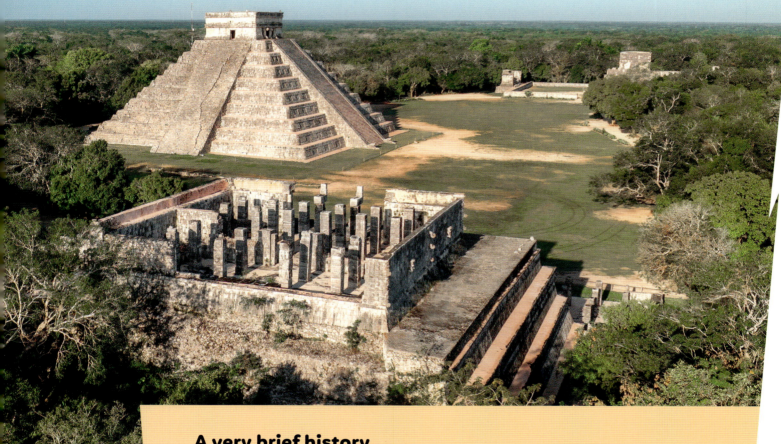

A very brief history
The city was founded by the Maya Itzá ("water magician") people around 435 CE. In the 900s, Toltec people from Central Mexico arrived, possibly as part of an invasion, and blended Maya and Toltec cultures. Around 1200, the city of Mayapán took over as the Maya center, and by the 1400s, Chichén-Itzá was largely abandoned.

City map
The biggest structure in the city is the Temple of Kukulcán, also known as El Castillo, at 78 feet (24 m) high. It is a **step pyramid** that functioned as a **temple** for Kukulcán, the feathered serpent god.

Playing ball
The ball court measures 554 feet (169 m) long—one-and-a-half times longer than a football field! Players used their hips, thighs, and upper arms to get a heavy rubber ball through a high stone hoop or into an end zone.

Stonework
Chichén-Itzá is famous for its intricate stonework. When the light hits it just right, a shadow slithers across El Castillo like a snake. The feathered serpent Kukulcán is carved all over the city, and one structure is dedicated to carvings and figures of eagles and jaguars.

FASCINATING FACT!

The Temple of Kukulcán has 365 steps, one for each day of the year. The calendar used by the Maya was based on the movement of the Sun, just as ours is today.

 FLORA AND FAUNA

SACRED CREATURES AND ADAPTED ANIMALS

Mexico's animal species are well-adapted to their particular environments. The desert creatures and plants can withstand heat and dry land, while rainforest wildlife helps keep wet **ecosystems** in balance, and ocean animals develop interesting techniques to find food.

DESERT DWELLERS

Greater roadrunner
These fast-footed birds can run up to 26 miles per hour (42 kph). They are well-adapted to the dry desert. To save water, they secrete salt through their eyes instead of urinating. Roadrunners pair up for life.

 FASCINATING FACT!

Roadrunners sometimes work together to hunt rattlesnakes. One distracts the snake by dancing in front of it while the other sneaks up behind it.

Black-tailed jackrabbit
These are actually hares and not rabbits. Rabbits burrow, while hares nest above ground. Hares also have bigger feet, which allows the jackrabbits to jump more than 10 feet (3 m). Their long ears help regulate their body temperature in the desert heat.

Desert bighorn sheep
Named for their enormous, curved horns, these sheep roam the deserts of northern Mexico. They can go days (even months, in cooler periods) without water, making them perfect for life in the desert. They can even eat cacti. The males use their horns to fight for territory.

Desert spiny lizard
These reptiles are **native** to the Chihuahuan desert. The males have a metallic blue underbelly. Everywhere else, they are camouflaged for rocky lands. Being cold-blooded, they work hard to keep warm. In winter, their skin darkens to absorb more heat.

IN THE WATER

Axolotl
Unlike other salamanders, these smiling **amphibians** never leave the water. They have feathery gills, a full-body fin, and webbed feet. Axolotls can regrow limbs without any damage or scarring. Many of the lakes they live in have been drained, leaving them extremely **endangered**.

Hogfish
Known as *pez perro* (dog fish) in Mexico, hogfish have long snouts with sharp canine teeth and long **dorsal** spines. They use their snouts to root out food such as clams and snails. All hogfish start life as female, then half the population turn into males as they grow older.

Gray whale
These aquatic mammals weigh up to 40 tons (36 tonnes). They eat by inhaling from the ocean floor and using a row of stiff spikes called a baleen to filter for food. In winter, they **migrate** more than 12,000 miles (19,312 km) from Alaska to the coasts of Mexico.

JUNGLE LIFE

Hercules beetle
These are among the largest flying beetles in the world. They can reach 8 inches (20 cm) long and the males have a curved horn that's longer than their main body. They are important to jungle ecosystems because they eat rotten fruit, which helps to recycle plant matter.

Resplendent quetzal
These unique birds live in the cloud forests. Their feathers are a vibrant green and red. During mating seasons, males grow a flowing blue tail up to 3 feet (1 m) long. Quetzals were considered sacred to the Aztecs. The god Quetzalcōātl is shown as a snake with the feathers of a quetzal.

Howler monkey
These are the loudest of the **primates**. Their calls can be heard up to 3 miles (4.8 km) away. Howler monkeys hardly ever touch the ground, preferring to stay up in the fruit- and leaf-rich treetops. Their long tails are strong enough for them to hang from.

15

PLENTIFUL PLANTS

Cactus
The lush Chihuahuan desert is home to 345 cactus species. They provide food and shelter for hundreds of species of animals. Cacti store water in their thick stems, and their spikes help reduce water loss from heat.

Agave
Agaves have thick leaves that reduce water loss in arid places. There are many varieties, some that grow to more than 10 feet (3 m) tall. Their sweet sap is often harvested and turned into agave syrup.

Dahlia
Dahlias are the national flower of Mexico. They were used by the Aztec people as food and medicine. There are more than 30 species of dahlia of all colors, from dappled blue to deep red.

Poinsettia
These plants are Mexico natives. Their leaves grow a deep green and red. The Aztecs grew poinsettias to use as medicine and make dyes. In the Náhuatl language used by the Aztec people, the name for poinsettia is *cuetlaxochitl*.

BRED AND ENDANGERED SPECIES

Fishing industry
Vaquitas are small **porpoises endemic** to Mexico. They have recognizable black lines around their eyes and mouths. There are fewer than 30 left in the wild. They have been killed off by fishing practices that use **gillnets**. A ban on gillnets was put in place in 2015 to try to conserve these unique creatures.

Habitat loss
Tapirs are stocky mammals related to horses. They have a trunk-like nose that they can move around to pluck leaves from branches. Their calves are patterned with white streaks. Tapirs have lost much of their forest and grassland homes to the farming industry. Despite conservation efforts, their numbers are continuing to go down.

Hairless hound
Xoloitzcuintlis are dark-skinned, hairless dogs. They are known to be intelligent and calm. They were first bred by the Aztec people and were considered sacred. In Aztec legend, they helped the god Xolotl guide souls through the underworld.

CULTURE

PEOPLE, SPORTS, AND ENTERTAINMENT

Mexico has a diverse population, with many cultures mixing together. It is also a culture that's very family oriented. This brings a rich variety of people, sports, pastimes, and celebrations!

PEOPLE

A mix of cultures
More than 60 percent of Mexican people today have a mix of Indigenous and European **heritage**. Around 30 percent identify as mostly or wholly Indigenous. The Afro-Mexican community, whose **ancestors** were mostly brought to Mexico as enslaved people by the Spanish, makes up about 2 percent.

Indigenous languages

There are at least 68 different Indigenous peoples in Mexico that speak hundreds of language **dialects** between them. The biggest group is the Nahua who speak the Náhuatl language. In Náhuatl, hello is *Pialli*.

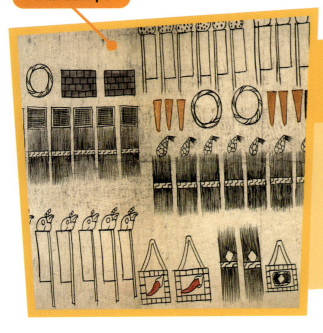

Nahua pictorial manuscript

 FASCINATING FACT!

The Aztecs spoke Náhuatl and referred to themselves as Mexica. The origins of the term Aztec are not fully known. Indigenous writers used the term *aztecatl* for members of the Aztec Empire.

Names

Many people in Mexico follow a Spanish naming system where each person has at least three names: a given name, their father's family name, and their mother's family name. Some people even have two given names!

Amada
(Given name)

López
(Father's family name)

Hernández
(Mother's family name)

ENTERTAINMENT

Lotería
This game is a bit like bingo. There are 54 cards in a pack, with a different picture on each. Players get a grid showing 16 images that match some of the cards. Cards are then drawn from the pack. If a card image matches an image on your grid, you mark it. The first to get a line of four wins.

Birthday parties
Birthday celebrations are family-centered, joyful events that are full of music and food. There is often a *piñata*: a paper model filled with candy that children hit open with sticks. Extra big celebrations are had when children turn 3, called *presentación de tres años*, and when girls turn 15, known as *quinceañera*.

Arts and crafts
Crafts are a common family activity. *Cartonería* is the art of papier-mâché, where paper is mixed with a paste of water and flour to make sculptures. *Papel picado* is the art of creating patterns in paper by poking or cutting holes in decorative shapes.

SPORTS

Rodeo
Called *charrería* in Spanish, this is the national sport of Mexico. Horse-riders show off different skills with horses and cattle. There are different events, including bull-riding (*jineteo de toro*); skirmish (*escaramuza*), where teams of women ride to music; and forefooting (*manganas a pie*), where someone tries to lasso a horse's front legs.

Wrestling
Known as *lucha libre*, Mexican wrestling is done in bright costumes and masks. Two wrestlers (*luchadores*) grapple in a ring. To win, they must pin their opponent for three seconds, knock them out of the ring, or get them to give up. Each wrestler wears a unique mask.

Soccer
The most popular sport in Mexico is soccer (*fútbol*). The top league is Liga MX, which has 18 teams. There is also a league for *fútbol rápido*—fast soccer, played inside a walled arena with 5 or 6 players on a team.

FIND OUT!

Two of the teams in Liga MX are known by the nicknames Cruz Azul and Chivas. Can you find out which areas these clubs are from?

Answer: Mexico City and Guadalajara

RELIGION

BLENDING OF BELIEFS

The most wide-spread religion in Mexico is Catholicism, which is a type of Christianity. Often, Indigenous beliefs and Christian beliefs are mixed together. Catholic churches have carvings in Indigenous designs, and Indigenous rituals will sometimes involve Christian saints.

Catholicism

When the Spanish invaded Mexico, they brought Catholicism. Catholics believe in a single god and worship that god's son, Jesus Christ. Catholics also follow the Pope, a religious leader in Rome who is the head of the Catholic Church. More than 75 percent of Mexicans identify as Catholic.

Basilica of Our Lady of Guadalupe

Syncretism

This term means the blending of two or more **belief systems**. In Mexico, many Indigenous people follow the Catholic religion alongside their own beliefs. For example, the Catholic saint Our Lady of Guadalupe is tightly connected to Tonantzin, a Náhuatl term meaning "our beloved mother" which represents several Aztec goddesses.

Indigenous belief systems

There are many different Indigenous beliefs and practices in Mexico. The Maya believe that everything is connected and emphasize the importance of harmony with nature. The Huichol make **pilgrimages** to a sacred desert area called Wirikuta and worship gods of nature. The Zapotec honor their ancestors.

Aztec and Maya influence

The ancient Aztec and Maya peoples had sophisticated belief systems tied to nature and the movements of the Sun, Earth, and other **celestial** beings. The Aztecs worshipped Huitzilopochtli, god of the Sun, and Chalchiuhtlicue, goddess of rivers and lakes. Maya gods included Chac, god of rain, and Itzamná, the creator god.

NATIONAL HOLIDAYS AND FESTIVALS

FAMILY, FUN, AND FIESTAS

Mexico has eight public holidays and many more parties (*fiestas*) and festivals. Holidays and other celebrations are often family occasions. They are full of music, joy, color, and hand-made crafts.

PUBLIC HOLIDAYS

Candlemas Day (Día de la Candelaria)
This is a Christian holiday on February 2 celebrating Mary, the mother of Jesus Christ. It also has ancient Aztec roots and marks the change from winter to spring. People eat a corn patty called a *tamal*.

Ofrendas

Independence Day (Día de la Independencia)
This celebrates Mexico's independence from Spain. On September 16, 1810, a priest named Miguel Hidalgo rang the church bells and began the independence movement. Today, people feast, wave flags, and set off fireworks on September 15. September 16 is a holiday.

Day of the Dead (Día de los Muertos)
On November 1 and 2, lively festivals are held that celebrate people who have passed. Families set up tables with *ofrendas* (offerings) of sugar skulls, pictures of loved ones, candles, and favorite foods. People dressed as skeletons parade through the streets.

FESTIVALS

Three Kings Day (Día de Los Tres Reyes Magos)

This day on January 6 marks the end of the Christmas season. A sweet, ring-shaped bread called *rosca de reyes* is eaten. Inside one of the slices, a small doll is hidden. If your family gets the slice with the doll, they have to make the *tamales* for Candlemas Day.

Guelaguetza

This is an Indigenous festival held in the state of Oaxaca in July. It celebrates the different Indigenous groups of the region with traditional dress, dancing, food, and music. The name Guelaguetza is from the Zapotec language and loosely means "gift" or "offering."

People's Day (Día de la Raza)

In some countries, this date (October 12) celebrates the day that Europeans arrived in the Americas. In opposition to the harm done by **colonization**, Mexico instead celebrates the cultural fusion of Spanish and Indigenous heritage.

FOOD AND DRINK

MEXICAN MENUS

Mexican food is full of flavor, spice, and color. Major ingredients include rice, beans, corn, and chili. Mexico is particularly famous for its street foods, called *antojitos*. These are dishes cooked in stands and trucks in the street, and they're bursting with flavor.

Mole
This is a smoky, spicy sauce made from chilis and spices. It can be made red (*mole rojo*) by using red chilis, green (*mole verde*) using green chilis and tomatoes, or black (*mole negro*) using chocolate. Mole is served with meats, vegetables, and a variety of dishes.

Mole

Tacos
These are small round tortillas topped with delicious fillings, like meat, beans, and vegetables. Tacos are a favorite street food because they are so easy to eat with your hands! Just fold the tortilla over the fillings and munch away.

Tacos

Pozole
This traditional soup is made from hominy (dried corn kernels) and meat in a broth of spices and chilis. The name comes from the Náhuatl word for hominy: *pozolli*.

Agua fresca
Meaning "fresh water," this is a fruity, refreshing drink made by blending fruit with water and sugar. Some popular Mexican flavors are hibiscus, watermelon, and tamarind.

Tamales
This dish has been around for 10,000 years or more. A *tamal* is a steamed patty made of masa (a dough made from corn) with fillings of cheese, beans, meats, or chilis.

Chilaquiles
This is a breakfast dish of fried tortillas in a red or green chili sauce. Often, beans and eggs are added.

Here are some popular Mexican sweet treats:

Churro
Fried dough sprinkled with sugar and cinnamon.

Tres leche cake
A cake soaked in three types of milk.

Concha
A sweet bread roll with a crunchy sugar coating.

Horchata
A drink made from rice soaked in water with cinnamon.

RECIPE

CHILAQUILES

This is a simplified *chilaquiles* recipe that uses store-bought tortilla chips so you don't have to fry your own. This makes 3 servings, with about 12–15 chips per person.

CHILI CHOICES

You can use guajillo chilis, jalapeño peppers, or serrano peppers—or whichever chilis you can find. Add more chilis if you like it spicy, or remove the seeds to make it milder.

Ingredients
- Around 35–45 tortilla chips
- 4 Roma tomatoes, chopped
- ½ a large yellow onion, chopped
- 1 medium jalapeño, sliced
- 2 cloves of garlic, minced
- 1 ¼ cups (300 ml) of low-sodium vegetable broth
- ½ tsp. of salt
- ½ tsp. of ground black pepper
- ½ tsp. of dried oregano

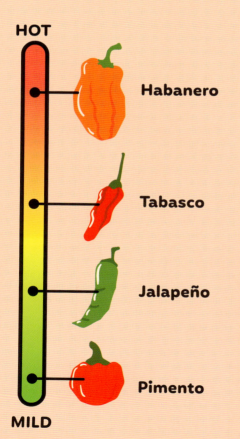

28

Ask an adult to help you with the chopping. If you touch the peppers, be careful not to touch your eyes afterward. Peppers can sting!

Method

1. Add the chopped tomatoes, onion, jalapeño, and garlic to a large skillet. Add the broth and bring it to a medium-high heat.
2. When it starts to boil, turn it down to medium-low. Let the vegetables simmer for about ten minutes, or until the tomatoes and peppers are cooked and soft.
3. Let the mixture cool. When it is no longer hot, pour it in a blender and blend until it's smooth (you could also use a stick blender instead). Then add it back to the pan and add the salt, pepper, and oregano.
4. Simmer the sauce on a medium-low heat for five to ten minutes until it starts to get a bit thicker.
5. Add the tortilla chips, but stop if the chips will no longer fit into the sauce. Stir them well so they are all coated in the sauce.
6. Let the chips heat through with the sauce for two or three minutes, then take it off the heat.
7. Serve immediately! You don't want the chips to get soggy. Add some of the topping suggestions.

TOPPINGS

Add any of the following to your *chilaquiles*, or get creative and add your own ideas.

- Avocado slices
- Queso fresco
- Fried egg
- Black beans

Queso fresco is a kind of soft, mild cheese. If you're adding beans, cook them separately or add them in step 3.

HOME, WORK, AND SCHOOL

LIVING, LEARNING, AND EARNING

Homes in Mexico tend to be colorful and many people live in family groups. In bigger cities like Mexico City, most people will live in apartments rather than houses. In **rural** areas, schools are smaller and might have fewer than 100 students. In cities, some schools are so busy they have a morning shift and an afternoon shift!

Hacienda style

City of Guanajuato

Types of home
There are many different styles of homes in Mexico. Adobe houses are made from a mixture of clay, earth, and water and have smooth, unbroken walls. Spanish hacienda-style homes are often light-colored and have small windows, tiled floors, and white walls. They are built for hot climates. Many homes are decorated colorfully with blue and terracotta tiles.

Going to school

In Mexico, school is compulsory between the ages of 6 and 18. There are general high schools as well as technical high schools that teach skills for certain jobs, like mechanic or engineer. Teachers are usually called *maestro* (for a man) or *maestra* (for a woman) followed by their first name.

Elementary school:
6–12 years old

Middle school:
12–15 years old

High school:
15–18 years old

Farming

Mexico is a huge supplier of fruits and vegetables, like tomatoes, strawberries, peppers, and onions. Most of its produce goes to the USA, but it also **exports** to the rest of the world. Mexico is the world's largest supplier of avocados. More than 6 million people work in the farming industry in Mexico.

Growing industry

The **aerospace** industry is one of the fastest growing sectors in Mexico. They make things like airplane bodies and helicopter parts. They also work on research and design for engines and turbines and specialized materials for aircraft. About 60,000 people in Mexico work in aerospace, and there are more jobs available each year.

SCHOOL DAY DIARY

AMADA'S DAY

Name: Amada López Hernández
Age: 11
Lives: Puebla
Family: Mom, Dad, Carlos (brother), and Luciana and Maria (twin sisters)

Buenos días! I am Amada and this is my day at school.

I get up at 6:45am and get washed and dressed. At my school we wear a white shirt and grey skirt or pants.

I help my mom with the twins while my brother makes breakfast.

We are having scrambled eggs with black beans, except the twins, who are only one-and-a-bit years old.

Carlos goes to high school round the corner from me, so he walks me and my best friend Silvia to school every day. It's Monday, so we have the flag ceremony first thing. That's when we gather in the playground to sing the national anthem, say the oath of allegiance (*juramento a la bandera*), and salute the flag.

Then we go to the classroom at 8:15am. We have our own individual desks and Silvia and I sit next to each other. Our teacher, Maestro Camilo, arrives. Our first class is Spanish (*Español*).

Since it is our last year at elementary school, we are working on a scrapbook of our memories. Maestro Camilo asks us to write a poem about our best memory of school. Mine is going to be from second grade when I met Silvia.

We have math next. We work in pairs, which is lucky for Silvia because I am great at decimals. Then it's time for recess. Silvia and I play jump rope with our friend Gabriela, then we sit in the shade to chat and eat mango.

$$1.2 + 5.9 = ???$$

After recess, we have social science. We are learning about the Battle of Puebla. This was when a French army tried to invade our city in 1862, but we beat them! It was a big deal because there were more of them, and they had better supplies. We celebrate it on Cinco de Mayo.

> Cinco de Mayo: Anniversary of the Battle of Puebla celebrated on May 5 in some areas of Mexico.

We have music class with the music teacher, Maestra Rita. We are learning how to manage our breathing properly when we sing. Before our last class, we have a quick lunch break. Today I have a *torta* with cheese and beans I brought from home. Our last class is PE. We are playing volleyball this semester.

> *Torta*: A bread roll sandwich with fillings.

Before we pack away, Maestro Camilo tells us what to do for our homework (write a presentation on a book we've been reading). Then Silvia's dad comes to pick us up because Carlos hasn't finished school yet. We walk home together, laughing while we practice our breathing from music class.

I get changed out of my uniform and my mom gives me some leftover tortilla soup (*sopa de tortilla*). I help get the twins changed, then I do my chores before I go to my room to work on my homework.

When Dad and Carlos are home, we sit together for dinner. Tonight, we're having *enchiladas* with *nopales* (cactus).

Sometimes after dinner, we play games. But tonight, I go to my room. I'm working on a secret art project for my cousin's *quinceañera* in a few weeks' time.

Enchiladas: Tortillas rolled around vegetables or meat and covered in a warm sauce.

When it's time for bed, I brush my teeth, and my mom and dad come to say goodnight. *Buenas noches!*

Quinceañera: 15th birthday celebration.

HISTORY

CIVILIZATIONS AND CIVIL WARS

Complex societies have existed in Mexico for thousands of years. The Olmec in the south were the first, at least 3,000 years ago. One of the earliest cities was Teotihuacán, with more than 125,000 people. After that, civilizations like the Aztec, Maya, and Zapotec dominated with huge empires. These civilizations farmed, traded, and developed political systems, writing and math systems, and ball games.

Olmec Colossal Head

Emerging powers

From about 700 BCE, the Maya and Zapotecs were the biggest powers. The Maya were made up of many different Mayan-speaking groups who lived in a network of cities, such as Chichén-Itzá, Mayapán, and Tikal. Then in the 1200s, Mexica people from the north began to migrate south.

Aztec Empire

The Mexica built the city of Tenochtitlán and formed an **alliance** with two neighboring cities, forming the powerful Aztec Empire. The Spanish arrived in 1519. They allied with the Tlaxcaltecan people, mortal enemies of the Aztecs, and attacked Tenochtitlán. In 1521, they defeated the Aztec city. This began 300 years of Spanish rule, Catholic conversion, and the importing of enslaved people from Africa.

Wars and revolutions

In 1810, a priest named Miguel Hidalgo led an **uprising** that began the War of Independence. Mexico became independent in 1821. During the Mexican–American war (1846–1848), Mexico lost land in the north to the USA. In 1910, the people rebelled against a corrupt government. This became a **civil war** known as the Mexican Revolution that lasted 10 years.

Twentieth century and today

Mexico enjoyed an **economic** boom in the mid-20th century. However, there was still a lot of inequality between the rich and poor, and between white Mexicans and Indigenous Mexicans. Today, Mexico is one of **Latin America's** largest economies. It continues to strive for stability and equality.

Chichén-Itzá

Hernán Cortés, conqueror of Tenochtitlán

Miguel Hidalgo

Guanajuato

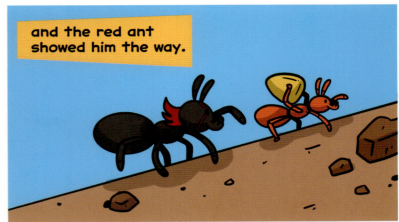

He returned with a kernel of corn.

The storm summoned Nanahuatl...

and Nanahuatl cracked open the Mountain of Sustenance.

Fetch the food!

The Tlaloques returned with corn of all colors for the humans to plant and grow.

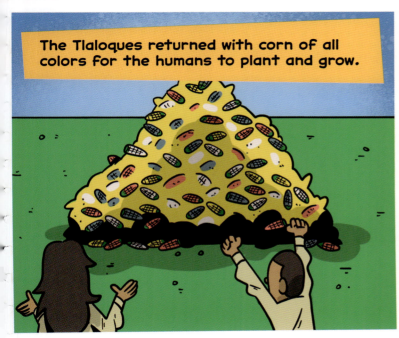

Today, corn can be white, yellow, red, and blue, just like the Tlaloques.

VOCABULARY BUILDER

A DAY IN TENOCHTITLÁN

Tenochtitlán was the capital of the Aztec Empire from around 1325 to 1521. Hundreds of thousands of people lived and worked there, and people from neighboring towns came to trade and worship. Here is an account of Tonauac, a young boy in the 1400s who is visiting Tenochtitlán for the first time.

Map of Tenochtitlán

The city is in the middle of a huge lake. To get there, we walk on a long strip of land called a causeway. Sometimes there are bridges that let boats go beneath us. We walk past *chinampas*—floating farms in the lake—before we reach the end. The city is huge!

The streets are full of people. There are lots of boats in the canals, too. Porters take food and goods from the boats to the market. We go to the **artisan** part of the marketplace. My dad is trading for some tools for his woodworking. Merchants are selling everything, from cacao and maize to bright clothes and colorful pottery.

Next, we go to the center to see the temple and the emperor's palace. We don't get close, but I see priests in their feathery headdresses walking across the white courtyard. We go to the ball court next. The athletes are getting ready to play. On our way out, we pass a steaming *temazcal* (bath house) and a big school, bigger than mine back home. Back on the causeway, we pass a line of soldiers returning to the city.

Templo Mayor (Great Temple)

What do people do?
artisan, athlete, ball player, emperor, farmer, merchant, potter, porter, priest, soldier, teacher, trader, woodworker

Aztec ceramic pot

What structures do you see?
ball court, bath house, bridge, canal, causeway, courtyard, farm, marketplace, palace, school, temple

Pick an ancient city you've learned about in school. It can be anywhere in the world. Imagine you are visiting the city for the first time and write about what you see and hear.
- What jobs are people doing?
- What buildings can you see?

GLOSSARY

Active volcano A volcano that has erupted in the last 10,000 years or that shows signs that it could erupt in future.

Aerospace Technology related to flight and space.

Alliance An agreement between peoples to work together.

Altitude Height above sea level. High altitudes are often in the mountains.

Amphibian A cold-blooded animal that can live both in and out of water, such as a frog or newt.

Ancestor A person you are related to who lived a long time ago.

Arid Dry and barren and getting little rain.

Artisan Someone whose job or trade requires skill with their hands, like a carpenter or potter.

Aztec Indigenous Náhuatl-speaking people in Mexico prior to the invasion of the Spanish.

Belief system A set of ideas, values, and stories that influence the way you live your life.

Biodiversity Variety in plant and animal life.

Celestial Relating to the sky.

Civil war A war between people who live in the same country.

Civilization A complex society involving things like technology, trade, industry, and systems of politics.

Colonization The act of taking control of a land and settling by force, often displacing people who already exist there.

Desert A dry landscape without much vegetation that is usually very hot during the day.

Dialect A variety of a language that is used in a particular area.

Dorsal On or near the back of an animal.

Economic Related to money and the economy.

Ecosystem A community of plants, animals, and other environmental factors that exist together with relationships and interactions that affect each other.

Empire A group of nations, lands, or countries ruled by one authority in power.

Endangered At risk of extinction.

Endemic Native to a specific area or country and mainly or only found in that area or country.

Export Something sold from one country or region to another country or region.

Gillnet A fishing method using a vertical wall of netting. This can often trap fish and other creatures that were not intended to be caught.

Indigenous people The earliest inhabitants of a land or those who inhabited a land before colonists arrived.

Heritage History, traditions, beliefs, and practices that are inherited from the past.

Latin America Countries in the Americas that speak Spanish or Portuguese.

Maya Indigenous peoples of Mexico and Central America who speak the Mayan language. This refers to both ancient Maya societies and Maya people living today.

Migrate To move from one place to another. For animals, this is usually done in groups and timed with seasons.

Mountain A high, steep landform.

Nahua Indigenous peoples of Mexico who speak Náhuatl.

Native Referring to a plant or animal that lives naturally in a place and has not been brought there.

Pilgrimage A journey to a holy place, often done on foot.

Population The people or organisms who live in a certain area. It can also mean the number of people or animals that live in a certain area.

Porpoise A small dolphin-like whale.

Primate A member of the animal family that includes monkeys, apes, and humans.

Rural Related to the countryside. A rural settlement is usually smaller and further out in the countryside than an urban town.

Step pyramid A triangular pyramid building for which each layer is a step.

Temple A religious building used for worship.

Tropical Related to regions around the equator, usually with hot and humid weather.

Uprising An act of rebellion, usually by people against those in power.

Volcano A vent in the Earth's crust where lava, hot ash, and gases erupt from or have erupted from in the past.

INDEX

A
aerospace industry 31
agaves 16
ants 38–41
avocados 29, 31
axolotls 14
Aztec
   beliefs 15, 23, 24
   Empire 4, 19, 36, 37, 42
   language 19
     see also Náhuatl
   legends 7, 8, 38–41
   people 7, 16, 17, 38–41

B
Belize 7
bighorn sheep 13
biodiversity 9
birthday celebrations 20, 35
black-tailed jackrabbits 13
butterflies 9

C
cacao 5, 42
cacti 7, 13, 16, 35
Candlemas Day 24, 25
Catholicism 22, 23, 24, 37
cenotes 9
Chichén-Itzá 5, 10–11, 37
Chihuahua state 4
Chihuahuan desert 5, 9, 13, 16
chilaquiles 27, 28–29
chilis 26, 27, 28
chocolate 5, 26
civilizations 4, 5, 36
cloud forests 5, 9, 15
corn 24, 27, 38–41
Cortés, Hernán 37
crafting 20, 24
culture 18–21

D
dahlias 6, 16
Day of the Dead 24
deserts 4, 5, 9, 12, 13, 16, 23
dialects 19
drinks 5, 27

E
economy 37
ecosystems 12, 15
education 31
empires 4, 7, 19, 36, 37, 42
enchiladas 35
enslavement 18, 37
endangered animals 14, 17
entertainment 20
exports 31

F
families 18, 19, 20, 24, 30
farming industry 9, 17, 31
fauna 9, 12–15, 17
festivals 25
fishing 17
flora 16
food, for animals 12, 14, 16, 38–41
food, for humans 10, 20, 24, 25, 26–27, 31
forests 4, 5, 8, 9, 12, 15, 17

G
gillnets 17
gods and goddesses 7, 11, 15, 17, 23, 38–41
gray whales 14
greater roadrunners 12
Guatemala 7
Guelaguetza 25

H
hairless dogs 17
Hercules beetles 15
Hidalgo, Miguel 24, 37
history 36–37
hogfish 14
houses 30
howler monkeys 15
Huitzilopochtli 7, 23

I
Independence Day 24
Indigenous beliefs 22–23
Indigenous languages 7, 16, 19, 37
Indigenous people 18, 19, 25, 37

K
Kukulcán 11

L
languages 7, 16, 19, 37
legends 7, 8
Lotería 20

M
maize 38–41, 42
Maya 5, 10, 11, 36, 37
   beliefs 23
   Empire 4
   language 7
Mayapán 10, 37
Mexican flag 6, 7
Mexican Revolution 37
Mexican–American war 37
Mexico City 4, 6, 7, 30, 37
migration
   of people 37
   of whales 14
mole (food) 26

N
Nahua 19
Náhuatl 7, 16, 19, 23, 27
naming system 19

O
ocelots 9
Olmecs 5, 36

P
People's Day 25
piñatas 20
poinsettias 16

Popocatépetl 8
public holidays 24

Q
Quetzalcōātl 15, 38–41
quetzals 9, 15

R
rattlesnakes 12
religions 22–23
rodeo 21

S
schools 30, 31
soccer (*fútbol*) 21
Spanish influences 6, 18, 25, 30
   see also Catholicism
Spanish invasion 7, 22, 37
Spanish language 6, 7
spiny lizards 13
sports 11, 21
street foods 26
sweet treats 27
syncretism 23

T
tacos 26
tamales 24, 25, 27
tapirs 17
temples 11, 43
Tenochtitlán 7, 37, 42–43
Teotihuacán 36
   terrains 8–9
Three Kings Day 25

Toltecs 10
tortillas 26, 27, 28, 29, 35

U
USA 7, 31

V
vaquitas 17
volcanoes 8

W
War of Independence 37
work 31
wrestling 21

X
Xoloitzcuintlis 17

Y
Yucatán 4, 7, 9
Yucatec Mayan 7

Z
Zapotecs 23, 25, 36, 37

ACKNOWLEDGMENTS

The publisher would like to thank the following for their kind permission to reproduce their photographs:

(Key: a-above; b-below/bottom; c-center; f-far; l-left; r-right; t-top)

Adobe Stock: Jacome 23cl, muratart 9br, pokku 16tl, Valente 21cl; **Alamy Stock Photo:** Cavan Images 15cr; **Dreamstime.com:** Agcuesta 25tl, Ernest Akayeu 21bl, Anastasiia Avksentieva 19tr, Bhofack2 27cl, Robert Briggs 20br, Byelikova 7tr, Carlosrojas20 26cr, Marcos Castillo 5tr, Jose De Jesus Churion 16cla, Elovkoff 30, Cesar Fernandez 34clb, Beata Jana Filarova 27b (cake), Gadost 24, Fernando Gregory 36, Patrick Guenette 37cra, Pavel Kudriavtsev 34-35b, Arlette Lopez 19br, Aleksandr Medvedkov 37br, Melitas 25bl, Nailotl Mendez 8, Moonkin 27b, Agnieszka Murphy 7b, Alexander Mychko 35cr, Veronika Oliinyk 28bl, Elena Pimukova 32b, Roywylam 4br, Sabelskaya 28br, Thiago Rocha Dos Santos 22, Scosens 13tl, Tartilastock 29tc, David Tonelson 27cla, Victor Torres 21tr, Tpanovaru 17b, Nattaporn Worakunpisad 29cb, Alona Zhitnaya 29ca; **Getty Images:** DEA / G. DAGLI ORTI / De Agostini 43cla, Moment / Matt Champlin 37tr, The Image Bank / John Elk III 11cra, The Image Bank / McDonald Wildlife Photography Inc. 17tr, Photo12 / Universal Images Group 19cl, Universal History Archive / Universal Images Group 11cl, Universal Images Group / Prisma 42cr; **Getty Images / iStock:** E+ / Oleh_Slobodeniuk 10; **Shutterstock.com:** Aberu.Go 6, Renata Alvarez 20cl, Aratehortua 31ca, Syana Artfanat 4-5 (Fishes), BearFotos 31clb, Mio Buono 5cb, bwx 7cl, clicksdemexico 25cl, James Michael Dorsey 14bl, Fresh_Vector 33bl, fukushima_insectarium 15tr, dg David Gonzalez 27clb, Kelp Grizzly Photography 13tr, Hajigrapher 17tl, Christopher M Hall 12, ItzaVU 27tl, George J 29c, KutuzovaDesign 34-35tc, Alan Mazzocco 30cr, mcarpizo 23br, Jen Mccormack 9tr, Anamaria Mejia 43cr, Narek87 14tl, Lorenza Ochoa 20tr, Charles T. Peden 13b, Denisse Pohls 14cl, primiaou 33tr, Kalah_R 31tr, Rawpixel.com 18b, Kittirat Roekburi 31crb, Prachaya Roekdeethaweesab 23tr, Yotha Somying 16bl, TheZAStudio 9cl, tim link 15br, Tanveer Anjum Towsif 26br, German Vizulis 37crb, Amelia Wong 16clb

Cover images: *Front:* **Getty Images / iStock:** Nirut Punshiri t; **Shutterstock.com:** ecstk22 cr, Granate Art bl; *Back:* **Dreamstime.com:** Marcos Castillo tl, Jose De Jesus Churion bl; **Shutterstock.com:** Narek87 cl

All of the books in the *DK Super World* series have been reviewed by authenticity readers of the cultures represented to make sure they are culturally accurate.